Cahoots Theatre Company and **David Sloan**
in association with **Park Theatre** present

Twilight Song

by Kevin Elyot

Twilight Song premiered at Park Theatre, London, on 12 July 2017

Twilight Song

by Kevin Elyot

Cast

HARRY	Philip Bretherton
SKINNER/GARDENER	Adam Garcia
ISABELLA	Bryony Hannah
BARRY/BASIL	Paul Higgins
CHARLES	Hugh Ross

Creative Team

Director	Anthony Banks
Designer	James Cotterill
Lighting Designer	Tim Lutkin
Composers & Sound Designers	Ben and Max Ringham
Dialect Coach	Elspeth Morrison
Dramaturg	Sebastian Born
Production Manager	Nick May
Company Stage Manager	Cassie Gallagher
Assistant Stage Manager	Leanne James

This production has been licensed by arrangement with The Agency (London) Ltd, 24 Pottery Lane, London W11 4LZ, email: info@theagency.co.uk

'It's Now Or Never' (Gold/Schroeder/Di Capua) courtesy of Rachel's Own Music/New Song Administration Ltd

Creative Team

Kevin Elyot | Playwright

Kevin was one of Britain's most esteemed playwrights and screenwriters, who made his name with the hit comedy *My Night with Reg*. He finished this new and final play shortly before he passed away in 2014. For *Reg*, Elyot won the Olivier and Evening Standard Theatre Awards for Best Comedy, the Writers' Guild Award for Best Play and a Critics' Circle Award, having previously won the inaugural Samuel Beckett Award for *Coming Clean*.

Theatre includes: *Coming Clean* (Bush); *Artists and Admirers*, a new translation from Alexander Ostrovsky (RSC at the Barbican); *My Night with Reg* (Royal Court/Criterion/Playhouse, recently revived at Donmar Warehouse/Apollo – Olivier Award nomination for Best Revival); *The Day I Stood Still* (National Theatre – Evening Standard Theatre Award nomination for Best Play); *Mouth to Mouth*, (Royal Court/Albery – Olivier and Evening Standard Theatre Award nominations for Best Play); *Forty Winks* (Royal Court) and a new version of Agatha Christie's masterpiece *And Then There Were None* (Gielgud).

His television drama *Killing Time* (BBC) won the Writers' Guild Award for Best TV Play or Film. He adapted *My Night with Reg* (BBC) for the screen, while other notable works include *No Night is Too Long*, adapted from the novel by Barbara Vine (BBC Film/Alliance); *Clapham Junction* (Channel 4); *Christopher and His Kind* (BBC); *Riot at the Rite* (BBC); *Twenty Thousand Streets Under the Sky* adapted from the novel by Patrick Hamilton (BBC) and many episodes of Agatha Christie's *Marple* and *Poirot* (ITV).

Anthony Banks | Director

Anthony studied English at King's College and directing at RADA. He was an Associate Director at the National Theatre for a decade until 2014, where he commissioned and developed a hundred new plays for NT Connections. Anthony leads workshops on directing new plays and contributes to books and journals about theatre.

Directing credits include: *Gaslight* starring Kara Tointon and Keith Allen (ATG/Smith & Brant/national tour); Patrick Marber's *After Miss Julie* starring Helen George (Theatre Royal Bath/national tour); Jim Cartwright's *Raz* (Trafalgar Studios/Assembly Festival/national tour); Bryony Lavery's *More Light*, Lucinda Coxon's *The Eternal Not* and Michael Lesslie's *Prince of Denmark* (National Theatre); Snoo Wilson's *Pig Night* (Menier Chocolate Factory); Mark Ravenhill's *The Experiment* (Soho/Berliner Ensemble); Lucinda Coxon's *Herding Cats* (Theatre Royal Bath/Hampstead); James Graham's *Bassett* (Bristol Old Vic); Dennis Kelly's *DNA* (national tour); Bryony Lavery's *Cesario* (World Shakespeare Festival/National Theatre/Tate Modern) and Tennessee Williams' *The Hotel Plays* (Grange & Langham Hotels, London).

James Cotterill | Designer

James trained at RADA in Technical Theatre before completing the Motley Theatre Design Course.

Recent designs include: *Fracked!* (Minerva/tour); *The Nap* (Crucible); *The War Has Not Yet Started* (Drum Plymouth); *Owen Wingrave* (BYO at Peacock); *The Events*, *Bully Boy* (Mercury Studio); *Blasted*, *Love Your Soldiers*, *Straight*, *The Pride*, *That Face* (Crucible Studio); *The Comedy of Errors*, *Much Ado About Nothing* (Shakespeare's Globe); *The Mighty Walzer*, *That Day We Sang*, *To Kill a Mockingbird*, *Good*, *Powder Monkey*, *A View from the Bridge*, *Mojo Mickybo* (Manchester Royal Exchange); *Hamlet*, *The Threepenny Opera*, *The Winter's Tale*, *An Enemy of the People*, *The Ancient Secret of Youth and The*

Five Tibetans, Early One Morning, Journey's End, Hobson's Choice, Long Day's Journey into Night, Macbeth, The Demolition Man (Octagon, Bolton); *As You Like It* (Jerwood Vanbrugh Theatre); *Accolade* (St James); *The Liberation of Colette Simple* (Spatfeather); *Moth* (Bush); *Smack Family Robinson* (Rose); *The Seven Year Itch* (Salisbury Playhouse); *The Flint Street Nativity* (Hull Truck); *The Wages of Thin* (Old Red Lion); *Not The End of the World* – winner of the Linbury Prize for Stage Design 2005 (Bristol Old Vic).

Tim Lutkin | Lighting Designer
Tim is a graduate of the Guildhall School of Music & Drama. He won the 2014 Laurence Olivier Award for Best Lighting Design for *Chimerica* at the Harold Pinter Theatre, London.

Other theatre credits include: *Les Blancs* and *Salome* (National Theatre); *The Rover, Candide* and *All's Well That Ends Well* (Royal Shakespeare Company); *The Crucible* (Old Vic); *Elf – The Musical* (West End/Plymouth/Dublin); *The Girls – The Musical* (West End); *Mickey and the Magician* (Walt Disney Imagineering®, Disney Studios Park®); *Strictly Ballroom – The Musical* (Toronto/WYP); *Philadelphia Here I Come!* (Donmar Warehouse); *Strangers on a Train* (West End); *The Full Monty* (West End/national tours); *Dynamo Live: Seeing is Believing* (Hammersmith Apollo/national & Australian arena tours); *Brontë* (Shared Experience); *Wondershow* (Roundhouse); *One Love: The Bob Marley Musical* (Birmingham Rep); *Close To You: Bacharach Reimagined* (West End/Menier Chocolate Factory); *Single Spies* (Chichester/national tour); *Impossible* (Original West End); *Once a Catholic* (Tricycle/Royal Court Liverpool); *Dynamo: The Power of X* (Copper Box Arena, London); *Rebecca* (Kneehigh/national tour); *Calendar Girls – The Play* (national tours); *Pan Oedd Y Byd Yn Fach* (Theatr Genedlaethol); *Children of the Smoke* (Glasgow Green/Glasgow 2014 Cultural Programme); *Hope Place* (Everyman, Liverpool) and *The Rime of the Ancient Mariner* (Royal Festival Hall).

Ben and Max Ringham | Composers and Sound Designers
Ben and Max are two-time Olivier Award nominated sound designers and composers. Recent theatre credits include: for the Jamie Lloyd Company, *Faustus* (Duke of York's) and *The Maids, The Ruling Class, Richard III, The Pride* and *The Hothouse* (Trafalgar Studios); *The Dresser* (Duke of York's); *Pygmalion* (Headlong); *Queen Anne, A Mad World My Masters* and *Little Eagles* (RSC); *La Musica* and *Ah, Wilderness!* (Young Vic); *Raz* (Assembly, Edinburgh); *The Mentalists* (Wyndham's); *We Want You to Watch, The World of Extreme Happiness, Scenes from an Execution, She Stoops to Conquer* and *Henry IV Parts I & II* (National Theatre); *2071, Adler & Gibb* and *NSFW* (Royal Court); *Dawn French and Fiction* (UK tour); *Blithe Spirit* (Gielgud/US tour); *The Full Monty* (Sheffield/Noël Coward); *Jeeves & Wooster in Perfect Nonsense* (Duke of York's); *A Midsummer Night's Dream* (Michael Grandage Company); *The Pride* (Royal Court/UK tour); *Lungs* (Berlin Schaubühne); *Ring* (BAC); *The Architects, Amato Saltone, What If…?, Tropicana, Dance Bear Dance* and *The Ballad of Bobby Francois* (Shunt); *The Duchess of Malfi* and *All About My Mother* (Old Vic); *Democracy* (Sheffield Crucible/Old Vic); *The Ladykillers* (Gielgud/Vaudeville/UK tour); *Phaedra* (Donmar Warehouse); *The Little Dog Laughed* (Garrick); *Three Days of Rain* (Apollo) and *Piaf* (Donmar Warehouse/Vaudeville/Buenos Aires).

Cast

Philip Bretherton | Harry

Philip is best known for playing Alistair Deacon in the long-running BBC sitcom *As Time Goes By* starring Dame Judi Dench and Geoffrey Palmer. He also played leading roles in *Coronation Street* (ITV), *Casualty* (BBC) and *Footballers' Wives* (ITV).

Recent stage credits include: playing Tony Benn in the one-man show *Tony's Last Tape* (Nottingham Playhouse, Edinburgh Fringe, and on tour including a special event at the House of Commons), as well as work at Salisbury Playhouse, Stafford Shakespeare festival, the Royal Exchange and Library theatres in Manchester, West Yorkshire Playhouse and the Citizens' Theatre Glasgow. He was an associate artist at Theatr Clwyd during Terry Hands' directorship and appeared there in *Somewhere in England* playing Tommy Handley, *God of Carnage*, *As You Like It*, *Blackthorn*, *Pygmalion*, *Blithe Spirit*, *Present Laughter* and *Noises Off*.

Adam Garcia | Skinner/Gardener

Adam Garcia is a two-time Olivier Award nominee, last seen on the London stage in Kenneth Branagh's *The Winter's Tale* as Lord Amadis opposite Dame Judi Dench (Garrick). Garcia starred in Kevin Elyot's BBC drama *Riot at the Rite* with Alex Jennings, and featured in Elyot's adaptation of *Agatha Christie's Marple – The Body in the Library* (ITV). He gained international recognition for his film roles including Kevin O'Donnell in *Coyote Ugly*, and Jason in *Riding in Cars with Boys* with Drew Barrymore.

Other theatre credits include: Bill Calhoun in *Kiss Me Kate*, directed by Trevor Nunn (Chichester/Old Vic – Olivier nomination); Fiyero in the original London cast of *Wicked* with Idina Menzel, directed by Joe Mantello (Apollo Victoria), having helped develop the role in early workshops in New York; Chip in *On The Town*, directed by Jude Kelly (Théâtre du Châtelet/London Coliseum); Don Lockwood in Jonathan Church's *Singin' in the Rain* (Australian tour); *The Exorcist*, directed by Sean Mathias (Birmingham Rep); *Where Do We Live*, directed by Richard Wilson (Royal Court); Tony Monero in *Saturday Night Fever* directed by Arlene Phillips (London Palladium – Olivier nomination); *Birdy* (Comedy); *Grease* (Dominion), and *Hot Shoe Shuffle* (Queens).

Adam appears in Kenneth Branagh's forthcoming film of *Murder on the Orient Express*. Previous film credits include: *Riding in Cars with Boys*; *Coyote Ugly*; *Nativity 3: Dude, Where's My Donkey?!* and *Love's Brother*.

In addition to his work with Kevin Elyot, other television credits include: *Genius* (National Geographic); Perry Benson in the acclaimed Australian political thriller *The Code* (ABC/BBC); Todd in *Camp* (NBC) and *Doctor Who* (BBC). Adam was a judge on *Got to Dance* (Sky 1) and the Australian version of *Dancing with the Stars*.

Bryony Hannah | Isabella

Bryony Hannah is best known for her lead role as Cynthia Miller in the BBC's blockbuster drama *Call the Midwife*. Bryony was Olivier Award nominated for her role as Mary Tilford in *The Children's Hour* (Comedy Theatre) opposite Keira Knightley and Elisabeth Moss, directed by Ian Rickson. She originated the role of Emilie in *War Horse* (National Theatre), directed by Tom Morris and Marianne Elliot.

Other stage credits include: *Blurred Lines*, directed by Carrie Cracknell (National Theatre); *Earthquakes in London*, directed by Rupert Goold (National Theatre/Headlong); *Breathing Irregular*, directed by Carrie Cracknell (The Gate); Perdita in *The Winter's Tale*, directed by Simon Godwin (Headlong); *Every Good Boy Deserves Favour*, directed by Tom Morris & Felix Barrett (National Theatre/Punchdrunk); *The Pillowman* (National Theatre on tour); *Norway Today* (Battersea Arts Centre), and *The Crucible* (Sheffield Crucible).

In addition to *Call the Midwife*, Bryony's television credits include: Cath in season two of *Unforgotten* with Nicola Walker and Sanjeev Bhaskar (BBC); Christine in *Dead Boss* (BBC), and Lynda La Plante's *Above Suspicion – Silent Scream* (ITV).

Film credits include: *Jupiter Ascending*, directed by The Wachowskis (Warner Bros.) and *Cemetery Junction*, directed by Ricky Gervais & Stephen Merchant (Point Productions).

Paul Higgins | Barry/Basil

Scottish-born actor Paul Higgins' career has spanned the worlds of television, film and theatre.

Paul has recently been seen on television in the BBC's hugely popular, award-winning police drama *Line of Duty* as CS Derek Hilton, with Thandie Newton and Vicky McClure. Earlier key roles include those in Armando Iannucci's political satire *The Thick of It* for the BBC; *Utopia*, co-starring Fiona O'Shaughnessy and Adeel Akhtar (Channel 4) and *Raised by Wolves* written by Caitlin and Caroline Moran (Channel 4).

Forthcoming film credits include: Stephen Frears' *Victoria & Abdul* with Judi Dench; *Apostle*, written and directed by Gareth Evans, with Michael Sheen and Dan Stevens, and *The Party's Just Beginning*, written, directed by and co-starring Karen Gillan. Previous film credits include: *In the Loop* directed by Armando Iannucci, in which he appeared alongside Peter Capaldi, Tom Hollander and James Gandolfini, and *Couple in a Hole*, with Kate Dickie, which was recently nominated for a British Independent Film Award (BIFA).

On stage, Higgins has performed in major productions including, most recently, *Temple* for the Donmar Warehouse, where he earlier appeared in *Luise Miller* and *The Cosmonaut's Last Message*. Earlier credits include: for the National Theatre, *The White Guard*, *Children of the Sun*, *Paul*, *An Enemy of the People* and *The Hare Trilogy*; *Macbeth* and *Conversations after a Burial* (Almeida); *Measure for Measure* (Royal Shakespeare Company); *A Midsummer Night's Dream* and *The Golden Ass* (Shakespeare's Globe); *Black Watch* (National Theatre of Scotland) and *Hope, Nightsongs, American Bagpipes* and *The Conquest of the South Pole* (Royal Court).

Hugh Ross | Charles

Hugh has had a long and distinguished career as an actor and director. He has worked for the RSC, the National Theatre, Sheffield Theatres, and frequently in the West End. He won a Time Out Performer Award for Cheek by Jowl's *Twelfth Night*, and was nominated for an Olivier Award for his performance in Stephen Sondheim's *Passion*.

Other recent theatre includes: *New World Order* (Brighton Festival/Barbican); *A Life* (Finborough); *Twelfth Night* (Sheffield/ETT); *Macbeth* (Trafalgar Studios); *Pyrenees* (Paines Plough/Tron/Menier Chocolate Factory) and *Hamlet* (Sheffield Crucible) with John Simm.

Television credits include: Scandi-drama *The Team* (recently on More4); *Marple, Poirot, Midsomer Murders,* and notably as Major Mungo Munro in *Sharpe* (ITV); *Psychoville* and *Absolutely Fabulous* (BBC) and many more.

Film credits include: *Sunset Song; The Iron Lady; Dorian Gray; Patriot Games; Trainspotting; Bronson,* and Clive Barker's *Nightbreed,* which has recently received cult status with the release of the Director's Cut.

Hugh broadcasts frequently for BBC Radio, Audible, and for Big Finish, including the hit series *Counter Measures.*

He directed the very successful revival of J.B. Priestley's *The Roundabout* (Park Theatre) which transferred to 59E59 Street in NYC in spring 2017 (Critics' Pick, *New York Times*).

Producers

Cahoots Theatre Company

As the producer for Cahoots, Denise Silvey has been awarded the Stage One Bursary and also the Stage One Start Up Fund in 2016 for the national tour of *Dead Sheep*. Andrew Mills joined Cahoots as General Manager in 2016.

Previous productions include: J. B. Priestley's *The Roundabout* (Park Theatre/59E59 Theaters, New York; *An Audience with Jimmy Savile* (Park Theatre and Edinburgh); *Dead Sheep* (Park Theatre/national tour); *Starting Here, Starting Now; Snap* and *Sick Dictators* (Jermyn St Theatre); *The Translucent Frogs of Quuup* (Edinburgh Festival/Ambassadors Theatre/King's Head); *Deco Diva* (59E59 Theaters, New York); *The Music of Andrew Lloyd Webber* (national tour); *Don't Call Me Nigel... an Evening with Graham Seed* (tour); *Burton* and *Clown in the Moon* (Edinburgh/St James Theatre); *Wilde Without the Boy, Rape of Lucrece, The Man Called Monkhouse* and *Hurricane Michael* (Edinburgh); *Deny Deny Deny* (Park Theatre); *Ferris and Milnes' Christmas Cracker* (Ambassadors Theatre) and *Twitstorm* (Park Theatre).

Future productions include *Looking for John* (Edinburgh Festival).

In addition to Cahoots Theatre Company, Denise Silvey is the Production Supervisor of the West End production of *The Mousetrap*.

Producer	Denise Silvey
General Manager	Andrew Mills
Assistant Producer	Anna Bolton
Marketing	Emma Martin
Accounts	June Basham

www.cahootstheatrecompany.com

David Sloan

David Sloan has worked for Assembly Festival, Tanya Link Productions and the Donmar Warehouse. For Assembly Festival, he produced *A Christmas Carol* starring Simon Callow in the West End and the new Jim Cartwright play *Raz* directed by Anthony Banks (Scotsman Fringe First Award), and was Production Coordinator for the London transfer of Yäel Farber's *Mies Julie*. For Tanya Link Productions, he general managed the new musical comedy *Miss Atomic Bomb* (St James Theatre). He completed the Society of London Theatre's Stage One Apprentice Scheme for New Producers at Sonia Friedman Productions and Act Productions, working on productions including *La Bête, Enron, The Children's Hour, Wicked* and *Legally Blonde*.

About Park Theatre

Park Theatre was founded by Artistic Director, Jez Bond. The building opened in May 2013 and, with three West End transfers, two National Theatre transfers and ten national tours in its first four years, quickly garnered a reputation as key player in the London theatrical scene. In 2015 Park Theatre received an Olivier nomination and won The Stage's Fringe Venue of the Year.

Park Theatre is a neighbourhood theatre with a global ambition.

We present world-class theatre, collaborating with the finest existing and emerging talent. We programme classics through to new writing, distinguished by strong narrative drive and powerful emotional content. We produce both in-house and in partnership with the most excellent existing and emerging producers, with whom we endeavour to provide an unparalleled level of support.

With a welcoming and nurturing environment we want Park Theatre to be accessible to everyone, within our diverse community and beyond – and through affordable ticket pricing and outreach programmes we aim to engage with those with little or no experience of theatre.

We aim to be a beacon for all and an ambassador for theatre worldwide.

★★★★★ 'A five-star neighbourhood theatre.' *Independent*

As a registered charity [number 1137223] with no public subsidy, we rely on the kind support of our donors and volunteers. To find out how you can get involved visit **parktheatre.co.uk**

Staff List

Artistic Director | Jez Bond
Executive Director | Rachael Williams
Creative Director | Melli Marie
Development Director | Dorcas Morgan
Artistic & Executive Assistant/Assistant Producer | Amy Lumsden
Finance Manager | Elaine Lavelle
Finance & Administration Officer | Judy Lawson
Sales & Marketing Manager | Dawn James
Deputy Sales & Marketing Manager | Rachel McCall
Box Office Supervisors | Natasha Chandra, Asha Cluer, Celia Dugua, Natasha Green, Bessie Hitchin, Georgina Jones, Jack Mosedale, Christopher Teesdale and Alex Whitlock
Venue and Volunteer Manager | Naomi Dixon
Duty Venue Managers | Barry Card, Shaun Joynson, Lorna Heap, Amy Allen
Technical Manager | Sacha Queiroz
Deputy Technical and Buildings Manager | Neal Gray
Access Programme Coordinator | Lorna Heap
Cafe Bar General Manager | Tom Bailey
Bar Staff | Sally Antwi, Gemma Barnett, Florence Blackmore, Grace Botang, Calum Budd-Brophy, Asha Cluer, Robert Czibi, Nicola Grant, Adam Harding-Khair, Philip Honeywell, Nigel Langley, Lasse Marten, Jack Mosedale, Emma Petrusson, Mitchell Snell, Amy Warren and Sam Williams.

Public Relations | Julia Hallawell and Nick Pearce for Target Live

President | Jeremy Bond

Ambassadors
David Horovitch
Celia Imrie
Sean Mathias
Tanya Moodie
Hattie Morahan
Tamzin Outhwaite
Meera Syal

Associate Artist
Mark Cameron

Trustees
Andrew Cleland-Bogle
Nick Frankfort
Robert Hingley
Mars Lord
Sir Frank McLoughlin
Nigel Pantling (Chair)
Victoria Phillips
Jo Parker
Leah Schmidt (Vice Chair)

With thanks to all of our supporters, donors and volunteers.

Twilight Song in rehearsal
Photography by Robert Workman

TWILIGHT SONG

Kevin Elyot

Characters

SKINNER
BARRY
BASIL
ISABELLA
CHARLES
HARRY
GARDENER

Setting

The play takes place in the same sitting room of a Victorian villa in North London during the early summers of 1961, 1967 and the present day.

A door leads into the rest of the house. A double-doored French window leads into the garden. The furniture includes a sofa and a 1920s mahogany gramophone cabinet. There's a fireplace with a mirror above it.

Doubling

SKINNER and GARDENER are played by one actor.
BARRY and BASIL are played by one actor.

Scene One

A grey drizzly afternoon in May, unseasonably dark. A barely discernible veil of mist shrouds the untidy room which seems to have seeped in from outside. A Bose radio/CD player stands on a table next to the 1920s mahogany gramophone cabinet. SKINNER (late forties), smartly suited, at the French window, looking out at the rain; BARRY (mid-fifties), watching him.

SKINNER. Live alone, do you?

BARRY. No. With my mother.

SKINNER. Where's she then?

BARRY. Dunstable.

SKINNER. Just the day for Dunstable.

He looks around.

Been here long, have you?

BARRY. Getting on for fifty years or more.

SKINNER. Fifty years, eh?

BARRY. All my life, actually.

SKINNER. Suffered any slippage?

BARRY. Well, I've had a few problems but –

SKINNER. Subsidence?

BARRY. Oh, I see. Yes, this whole area – you can't move for cracks.

SKINNER. Very nice though. You couldn't be better located.

BARRY. You think so?

SKINNER. Almost recession-proof.

BARRY. Well –

SKINNER. Believe me.

BARRY. Right.

A gurgling of water pipes from upstairs.

SKINNER. It used to be part of the Great Forest of Middlesex, you know.

BARRY. Had it?

SKINNER. Oh yes, I've done my homework. A case of having to now we're getting a bit more international. Americans love a little snippet like that: the Great Forest of Middlesex.

BARRY. I never knew there was one.

SKINNER. Of course it hasn't existed for years. Chopped down by Henry the Third.

BARRY. Henry the Third?

SKINNER. In the thirteenth century.

BARRY. Why would he go and do a thing like that?

SKINNER. Robbers, so they say.

BARRY. Really?

SKINNER. The place was swarming with them.

BARRY. Good heavens.

SKINNER. Ah well, *plus ça change*.

BARRY. Yes, quite.

SKINNER. That's the trouble with royalty: think they own the bloody place.

A sudden grating, cranking sound.

BARRY. That'll be the fridge. We've been meaning to get a new one but…

SKINNER. Your compressor needs replacing.

The sound continues.

BARRY. It'll stop soon.

They wait. It stops.

That's better.

SKINNER. Not that I've got anything against the present incumbent, God bless her. She's a diamond: solid, reliable, just like my Audi. I just wish she'd chill out a bit, know what I mean? Always looks like she's got a knob of ginger stuck up her arse.

BARRY. Can I get you anything?

SKINNER. Not while I'm on the job.

BARRY. No, of course.

SKINNER. What's she doing in Dunstable then?

BARRY. My mother?

SKINNER. Yes.

BARRY. She has an appointment.

SKINNER. An appointment in Dunstable, eh?

BARRY. She has one every Thursday.

SKINNER. Hospital, is it?

BARRY. Not exactly. In fact, she's doing pretty well, considering. I think I'll conk out before her what with this and that, and my heart's not too clever – that's what did for my dad. Have you got a mother, Mr Skinner?

SKINNER. Skinner, please.

BARRY. …Right.

SKINNER. No, I haven't. She died when I was a baby.

BARRY. Oh dear.

SKINNER. Didn't know anything about it, did I? Then my dad upped sticks and we went down under. He'd got a bit of money, see – I'm not sure how – and went through it like a tit in a trance. Ended up in Wagga Wagga.

BARRY. I've not heard of that.

SKINNER. About as exciting as Swindon on a wet Sunday.

BARRY. I thought you had a little twang.

SKINNER. Eh?

BARRY. Your accent, just a hint of… whatever.

SKINNER. Yeah. Clings like crabs.

BARRY. Were you there for long?

SKINNER. I was back here like a shot once they let me out of youth offenders'. Dad had drunk himself to death, see, and I went a bit off the rails.

BARRY. What had you done?

SKINNER. This and that, but I'm well-reformed now. I learnt all sorts in there: plastering, life skills, and a few positions even the Christian Brothers never got round to.

BARRY. You were taught by the Christian Brothers?

SKINNER. I'd swing for those cunts, pardon my French. Let your hair down, do you, Mr Gough?

BARRY. I'm sorry?

SKINNER. On a Thursday, when your mum's in Dunstable?

BARRY. Not exactly. I'm not the hair-letting-down type – although I used to… let it down. In fact, I let it down quite a bit… and even now, if I think about it, once in a while… I'll let the odd lock… drop.

SKINNER. You've got to live for the here-and-now, haven't you? No use putting it off.

BARRY. That's what Mother says. 'You're letting it slip away, Barry. One simply has to get on, get a grip.' She says it quite a lot, actually.

SKINNER. Sensible woman, your mother. Yeah, I can imagine you're a bit of a goer on the quiet.

BARRY. Well, I wouldn't quite say that…

SKINNER. Always the quiet ones.

BARRY. And I wouldn't say I'm that quiet.

SKINNER. So what do you do, if you don't mind my asking? Or are you one of the idle rich?

BARRY. No I'm not. I was given early retirement.

SKINNER. Happens a lot now, doesn't it?

BARRY. Yes. I worked in a pharmacy, the same one nearly all my life. The years I gave to that place… Mother wanted me to be a doctor but I never quite cut the mustard. I thought I'd made a fair enough compromise but she of course didn't, and all the time what I secretly wanted was to be a dancer.

SKINNER. Oh yeah?

BARRY. Then it transpired I had Policeman's Foot.

SKINNER. Nasty.

BARRY. It is. Intermittent, but very painful.

SKINNER. I once had a mate who wanted to be a bouncer.

BARRY. Really?

SKINNER. Yes, but he had Doorman's Knob.

BARRY. It's hard, isn't it? Thwarted ambition.

The water pipes gurgle again.

I sometimes think about getting a little job but it's not that easy, and the older you get, well… That's why I'm curious about the value in case we have to downsize.

SKINNER. So what do you do with yourself all day?

BARRY. Oh, I keep myself busy. Go out… stay in. I do see the odd exhibition or… friend, although… it's strange now wandering around London. It's full of memories: a restaurant, a park, a corner. That's where I did such-and-such with so-an'- so all those years ago, and of course they're not there any more. All dead or moved on. Like a cemetery.

SKINNER. Funny old place, isn't it? The other day I saw a bloke on one side of town, then the next day I saw him on the other. Imagine!

BARRY. But I wouldn't live anywhere else. I couldn't, not now, because of Mother.

SKINNER. Not exactly a barrel of laughs then.

BARRY. I don't think it was ever meant to be.

SKINNER. Certainly not round my gaff, I tell you.

BARRY. Do you have a family… Skinner?

SKINNER. Just the wife, and her bloody mother who's always sniffing around. I tell you, it's all moaning, misery and death in my house. That's all I got, Mr Gough. As soon as I walk through the door, I feel my balls shrivelling. Leave them to it, it's the only way.

BARRY. You don't have children?

SKINNER. No, thank God. Christ knows how they'd have turned out. (*Glancing out at the garden.*) Now that's odd: looks like you got a bit of a terrace out there.

BARRY. Yes, we have.

SKINNER. Intentional, like?

BARRY. No. We just ran out of…

SKINNER. Money?

BARRY. Interest, really. Thought it was a good idea, then… never got round to finishing it.

SKINNER. That is a pity, cos when the weather's nice, you could have sat out there with a little drinkie. Fancy, fifty years and no terrace. The missus wouldn't have let me get away with that.

BARRY. Does she keep you on a tight rein?

SKINNER. When she can. Now, I love my football, go to the match, have a bit of a kick-around some Sundays, but she says I'm neglecting her. I ask you! And you know what she did? Only went and burnt my boots.

BARRY. Oh dear.

SKINNER. Like a bloody brownshirt!

BARRY. Couldn't you buy some more?

SKINNER. I did, but they're hidden in my shed. I thought that was well beyond the pale, Mr Gough. How would you feel if someone burnt your boots?

BARRY. I don't have any.

SKINNER. Well peeved, I reckon.

BARRY. I never have had.

SKINNER (*re: ceiling*). Very nice bit of moulding up there. Nice bit of egg-and-dart, not too flash. Pity about the damp patch. You know what I think, Mr Gough? I think your mum's playing away.

BARRY. What?

SKINNER. Appointment in Dunstable? Pull the other one!

BARRY. No, I assure you, she's not... playing away, as you put it. She sees someone every Thursday.

SKINNER. That's what I'm saying.

BARRY. A spiritualist.

SKINNER. Oh.

BARRY. She... lost someone, you see, many years ago now, and she's never got over it. She'll do anything to try and make contact, even with the spirit world, in case he's passed over.

SKINNER. Right. Me and my big mouth.

He looks out of the window. The rain's heavier.

(*Re: the rain.*) It's coming down now.

SKINNER *watches it.* BARRY *watches him.*

Mate of mine, a deal younger than me, joined the army. Football mate, you know? He tried to get me to – get me out of the house, new life, new way of seeing things – but I couldn't face it.

BARRY. It has its downsides.

SKINNER. Ended up in Afghanistan.

BARRY. Good heavens.

SKINNER. Oh, he loved it out there. Said it made him feel alive for the first time in his life.

BARRY. Well, there you go.

SKINNER. But he didn't make it. When his coffin was carried out the plane, I had a lump just here – (*Indicating his throat.*) like a brick. And it wasn't because he was dead; it was because his wife was there with his little boy and his mum and dad, trying to hold themselves together, and I thought if I was in that coffin, who'd be there to cry for me?

BARRY. Your wife, your mother-in-law –

SKINNER. No one, and it was because of that I could have wept. What's the penalty for a wasted life, eh?

BARRY. But he didn't waste it; he died for something he believed in.

SKINNER. I mean me, Mr Gough. My life. Ever asked yourself that? It gets you sometimes, it really does.

He looks out of the window again. BARRY*'s at a loss, then:*

BARRY. You're surprisingly sensitive… for an estate agent.

SKINNER. It's getting dark already. I hate the night. Never know what's going on. Sometimes I wake up and can't breathe.

BARRY. Panic.

SKINNER. Yes, or the wife with her hand clamped over my face to stop me snoring – like *Alien*.

The grating, cranking of the fridge starts up.

(*Re: fridge.*) How do you live with that?

BARRY. You think this'd fetch a decent price then?

SKINNER. Victorian villa? This location? Worth its weight, Mr Gough, even in this state. So you're thinking of selling?

BARRY. Well… I'd like to know what I might be getting… whenever. Money is a little tight these days.

SKINNER. You'rc not kidding. The old estate agenting's been rough this past year or two.

BARRY. Everyone's feeling the pinch.

SKINNER. All in it together, eh? I don't think so! Fucking lard-arsed Etonians, if you'll pardon my French. Yes, Mr Gough, pretty rough it's been. I've had to take on a little bit extra to keep my head above water.

BARRY. What else can one do?

SKINNER. Think outside the box, that's the trick of it. Now a brickie mate of mine, he's taken up aromatherapy.

BARRY. I wouldn't have thought of that.

SKINNER. Exactly. You'd be surprised what people come up with. Round where I live, there's all these women stuck at home and they appreciate the occasional treat, Mr Gough. They like a bit of the old scented oil.

BARRY. And what do you do?

SKINNER. Fuck people. Now that's one nice fireplace you got there, Mr Gough. Yes, women, men. In my book, every hole's a goal.

BARRY. I must say, I'm rather taken aback.

SKINNER (*looking at the ornaments on the mantelpiece*). I thought I might be a bit long in the tooth, but you'd be surprised how many go for the maturer man. Do you have a partner, Mr Gough?

BARRY. Yes. My mother.

SKINNER. Man's best friend.

BARRY. You know, sometimes I think I should just get up and go, leave her to it, but I never do. I always find myself standing here like a child as if all the years that have passed were as nothing, craving her indulgence and awaiting her approval.

SKINNER. Hang on, man's best friend's a dog, isn't it?

He bends over to inspect a scuttle in the grate. BARRY *can't resist a peek.*

Very nice… oh yes, I like that. (*Straightening up.*) You've got some tasty artefacts, I must say.

The rain intensifies. SKINNER *looks out at it.*

Ne'er cast a clout, eh, Mr Gough?

BARRY. No…

SKINNER. Oh well, who knows what's round the corner, partner-wise?

BARRY. I'm afraid my sentimental side's somewhat muted now. The last time I felt more than the usual stirrings was in Venice. I'd gone with my mother for a long weekend, but she ate a dodgy clam and took to her bed. He was a waiter at the hotel and had that Italian twinkle that's quite hard to fathom. I took him for a very nice lunch that lasted till dusk, but even as we spoke, and the sun set behind the Salute, I felt that familiar disappointment as we slowly sank into the sludge.

SKINNER. Now that's somewhere I've always fancied – Venice. A touch of the Cornettos on a gondola.

BARRY. You should take your wife…

A look from SKINNER.

Perhaps not…

SKINNER (*re: the old gramophone*). Does this still work?

BARRY. Oh no, we haven't used it for years. It's a family heirloom, an ugly piece really. We've just never got round to getting rid of it. (*Re: the house.*) So you don't think we'd need to do it up then?

SKINNER. You'd be wasting your money, Mr Gough.

BARRY. Not even a coat of paint?

SKINNER. Not even a lick.

BARRY. Well, that's… most informative.

SKINNER. What I'm here for.

The rain pours.

BARRY (*with great difficulty*). I wonder, would you… would you ever consider…? I mean, might it be possible to… to see your way to… doing it with me… perhaps?

SKINNER *looks at him.*

SKINNER. Ooh, I don't know, Mr Gough.

BARRY. No, I understand. I do, really. I mean, why on earth would you fancy me?

SKINNER. Fancying doesn't come into it. I have catered for the older market. It's just the practicalities, you see. I feel a bit uncomfortable during office hours.

BARRY. Maybe another time…

SKINNER *thinks for a moment, then:*

SKINNER. Anything in particular you go for?

BARRY. No, I have… fairly catholic tastes.

Beat.

SKINNER. I know all about them, believe me.

BARRY. Although…

SKINNER. Yes, Mr Gough?

BARRY. I've often wondered…

SKINNER. Spit it out. You might as well get your money's worth.

BARRY. Well, my first encounter, a long time ago now, was with a gentleman I met in a pub in Bayswater: The Goat and

Monkey. He took me to a rather squalid boarding house, and after some prolonged and, I must say, expert foreplay, the next thing I knew, it was morning and he'd gone, and all I was left with was a circle of blood on the sheet. I tried to find him again but of course I never did.

SKINNER. To punch him in the mouth?

BARRY. Well, no. To see if we might do it again, actually, but this time with me conscious.

SKINNER. Right… So you fancy a bit of the old Goat and Monkey, then?

BARRY *nods briefly.* SKINNER *thinks for another moment, then:*

I'd do it for double the rate.

BARRY. That's alright. I popped to a cashpoint this morning.

SKINNER. And I can't guarantee a full-blooded performance. The old kidney-wiper doesn't automatically stand to attention these days.

BARRY. I've got a stash of Caverject that's highly efficacious – if you don't mind hypodermics.

SKINNER. Oh, I'm well used to needles.

BARRY. Good. I'm quite adept at injecting.

SKINNER. No kissing, mind.

BARRY. No.

SKINNER. Cos I really don't fancy you – (*Checking his watch.*) and I'll have to be gone by half-past.

BARRY. Yes.

He looks down at the gramophone, immensely self-conscious.

SKINNER. Right then, Mr Gough, better get cracking.

Blackout as Chopin's 'Étude Op. 10, No. 1 in C major' starts playing.

Scene Two

BASIL (*mid-forties*), *in exactly the same position as* BARRY *at the end of the previous scene, stands at the gramophone on which the Chopin is playing, lost in the music.* ISABELLA (*late twenties*) *and* CHARLES (*sixty-two*), *away from the gramophone, and* HARRY (*fifty-six*), *filling his pipe at the open doors of the French window, are listening with varying degrees of interest.* CHARLES, HARRY *and* ISABELLA *are in evening dress,* BASIL *isn't. All have drinks:* ISABELLA, *a gin and tonic; the men, tumblers of whisky. There are a few unpacked boxes from a removal firm piled against a wall. The Bose radio/CD player's gone. A late afternoon in May. Golden sunlight streams in. The record suddenly sticks. The sound of digging from the garden.*

BASIL. Damn!

He takes the stylus off the disc.

Always at the climax.

ISABELLA. That's because it's scratched.

BASIL. Those wretched removal men!

ISABELLA. It's always going to stick before the climax.

BASIL. They broke several things, you know, Uncle Charles.

CHARLES. That won't do.

ISABELLA. They were a little on the rough side.

CHARLES. Won't do at all.

HARRY. You should demand compensation.

BASIL. Don't worry, I will. (*Re: the record.*) Perhaps if I try again –

ISABELLA. No, Basil, put it away.

BASIL (*returning it to its sleeve*.) So infuriating.

ISABELLA. You'll just have to buy another.

BASIL. It is marvellous, though, isn't it?

CHARLES. Every time you play it.

BASIL. So uplifting.

ISABELLA. You really should get ready, you know.

BASIL. Don't you think, Harry?

HARRY. Very… light-fingered.

BASIL. Isn't she though?

HARRY. Polish, I believe?

BASIL. Hungarian, actually.

HARRY. As you know, old chap, I'm not that musical. Rough-and-tumble on the field's more my bag.

CHARLES. Although you have been known to enjoy the occasional trip to the theatre.

HARRY. Ah, well, I put that down to Fleur; she's more the arty type.

BASIL. And Uncle Charles.

CHARLES. I've always had something of a theatrical bent.

BASIL. You certainly have.

CHARLES. As Harry well knows. In fact, he's one of the few to have had the privilege of seeing me tread the boards.

HARRY. Not so sure about privilege.

CHARLES. Come on, old chap, I wasn't half bad. Remember the officers' mess panto?

HARRY. Hard to forget.

CHARLES. You were damned impressed by my Mother Goose. Nearly stopped the show.

HARRY. Someone should have.

ISABELLA. Did you ever think of taking it up professionally?

CHARLES. Good heavens, no. Medicine was my calling. That's where I felt I could do most good in this brief sojourn in the sun.

Beat. The sound of digging.

We haven't been to the theatre since last year, have we, Harry?

HARRY. That long, is it?

CHARLES. I wanted us to see *The Amorous Prawn*. I've always been such a great admirer of Evelyn Laye ever since *Lilac Time* –

BASIL. I think we may have heard this.

CHARLES. – but Harry insisted on catching Mr Hitchcock's new film *Psycho*.

HARRY. Fleur was at the Soroptimists' so I thought I'd take advantage.

CHARLES. Well, I didn't get it at all. Forty-five minutes in, poor Janet Leigh, our leading lady, mind, gets the chop –

HARRY. Several, in fact.

CHARLES. – and I could only think, whither are we bound? So out we trotted – popped to the club, didn't we, Harry? – and left Mr Hitchcock to his shenanigans.

HARRY. I can't help feeling we missed the point.

CHARLES. I don't know what's happening to people. I put it down to that frightful Mr Osborne. Do you remember that play we saw?

HARRY. Of course I do.

CHARLES. Some woman doing a pile of ironing and a young man ranting on about this and that. We barely lasted till the first interval. That's not what I go to the theatre for. If I want to see a woman doing a pile of ironing, I'll sit and watch the char.

BASIL. Bless you, Uncle Charlie.

CHARLES. Oh dear, am I being the most frightful old stick-in-the-mud?

HARRY. A little pusillanimous, perhaps.

ISABELLA. You're allowed to think whatever you wish, Charles. It's a free country, thanks to the likes of you. (*Confidingly*.) And I wouldn't be at all surprised if Basil didn't think exactly the same.

BASIL (*joining* HARRY *at the window and looking outside*). Works like a Trojan, doesn't he?

HARRY. A good man, no doubt about it.

They step outside, HARRY *clutching his Scotch and pipe*.

ISABELLA. There's something about him, isn't there?

CHARLES. Basil?

ISABELLA. Of course.

CHARLES. Yes, he's a good boy. Always has been. It's such a shame his mother and father aren't around to see all this. You've made him very happy, Isabella.

ISABELLA. He's made me very happy, Charles. This wonderful house, a little baby on the way. And he's a kind man, and – well, I can't believe how lucky I am. My mother was worried I'd end up on the shelf.

CHARLES. You're still so young.

ISABELLA. It's been such a whirlwind since meeting him. When he put the mask over my face with the ether, there was a look between us and I thought, 'Oh heavens, this might be it!', and then I floated off.

CHARLES. Do you miss your tonsils?

ISABELLA. I never think about them.

CHARLES. Better out than in.

ISABELLA. It was so touching the way he bought me little posies and gave me tokens. He's quite awkward with that sort of thing, as I'm sure you know.

CHARLES. Oh yes, really quite clumsy. Always was.

ISABELLA. But very endearing, and when he suddenly proposed – we were strolling through Green Park, a lovely evening just like this – well, I couldn't believe my ears, and I thought about it for a day, a week, and then I thought, why not? Isabella Matthews walking down the aisle on the arm of an anaesthetist. The most sensible decision I've ever made.

She drains her drink.

Oh dear, this is going to my head.

CHARLES. Shall I top you up?

ISABELLA. I'd better hold back if we're going for dinner.

CHARLES. Now are you sure you can afford it?

ISABELLA. Of course we can. We couldn't possibly have afforded this house without your help, and Harry was so generous with his legal expertise and finding that man to lay the garden. Dinner's the least we can do.

BASIL *and* HARRY *come back in.*

HARRY. It's coming on jolly well.

BASIL. All straight lines like a French garden.

ISABELLA (*taking a look out*). Oh yes! It'll look so lovely, and we can have drinks out on the terrace when it's nice.

BASIL. We don't actually have a terrace.

ISABELLA. Then we'll get one, silly boy! We'll have one built.

BASIL. Izzy thinks I'm made of money, don't you, darling?

He pecks her cheek and gives her a squeeze.

ISABELLA (*stiffening*). No squeezing now. We don't want baby popping out before time.

A momentary hiatus as she takes a cigarette. HARRY *lights it for her.*

How's your little boy getting on?

HARRY. He's not that little any more. Do you know, he's already nine?

ISABELLA. Is he really?

BASIL. Good heavens.

ISABELLA. I expect it broke Fleur's heart, leaving him at the school.

HARRY. He seems to be settling in well enough.

BASIL. Something I never managed. I couldn't stand the place.

CHARLES. But you were a gentler sort, Basil, and there's nothing wrong with that. Monty's more like his father.

HARRY. Should I take that as a compliment?

CHARLES. What a dreary old world this would be were we all cut from the same cloth!

HARRY. Poor old Fleur's found it all rather exhausting. The change will do her good.

ISABELLA. She'll miss him dreadfully.

HARRY. Of course she will, but she's not as young as she was. We were late starters at this parenthood lark.

CHARLES. Yes, you took us all by surprise.

ISABELLA. Well, I think it's absolutely wonderful. Now Basil, you have to get ready.

BASIL. Yes, matron, I'm going now.

ISABELLA. Please don't call me that.

BASIL (*to* CHARLES *and* HARRY). Better get my gladrags on.

ISABELLA. I'll give you a hand. (*To* CHARLES *and* HARRY.) Do excuse us.

ISABELLA *leads* BASIL *out of the room.* HARRY *gives* CHARLES *a look, then looks out of the French window and takes a deep breath.*

HARRY. An English summer, a decent Scotch, a full pipe and an Etonian at the helm. Bloody marvellous! Down the hatch!

He drains his glass and goes to the drinks trolley for a top-up.

CHARLES. Do you think you should?

HARRY. You're not in your surgery now, doc. Yes, good old Mac! You see, you've got to be straight with people. Gaitskell's decent enough, I suppose, but you can't pull the wool over people's eyes. They're not stupid – most of them anyway. Something for nothing? Tommyrot! Everything comes at a price in this life...

He falters.

CHARLES. Are you alright, Harry?

HARRY. Yes, of course I'm alright. That's why Labour got a bloody nose at the last ding-dong, but I'm damned sure there are elements within their ranks that enjoy opposition, that enjoy sniping from the sidelines. Buggers everything up for the rest of them. Still, let 'em get on with it, that's what I say. Leave the grown-ups in charge, eh?

CHARLES. Why not sit for a minute?

HARRY. I'm fine as I am.

CHARLES. Have a breather.

CHARLES pats the sofa next to him. HARRY reluctantly sits.

You push yourself too much. You should take care. We're not youngsters any more.

HARRY. When I want a consultation I'll make an appointment.

CHARLES. Unless something's wrong. Is there, Harry? Is something wrong?

HARRY. Nothing's wrong.

CHARLES. Well, something's changed. We don't chum up as we used to, that's for sure. Our little trips to the theatre, suppers at the club. What's happened?

HARRY. My son has happened. I'm a father.

CHARLES. You've been a father nearly ten years and I couldn't be happier for you, but I know you, Harry. Something's up and I've a right to be told.

HARRY. 'A right'? I don't think so, old chap.

He swigs his drink. CHARLES *puts a hand on his knee.*

(*Flicking it away.*) For God's sake, man!

CHARLES. Sorry…

HARRY. What are you thinking of?

CHARLES. Sorry… I'm sorry…

HARRY takes another swig. Beat.

It's good to see you anyway.

HARRY. Yes, yes…

CHARLES. Basil and Isabella seem jolly happy.

HARRY. Yes, don't they?

CHARLES. And Fleur: on good form, is she?

HARRY. Oh yes, keeps herself busy doing this and that.

CHARLES. And Monty…

HARRY. Settling in.

CHARLES. Yes.

HARRY. As I said.

Beat.

Well, I suppose we'd better get ourselves tip-top…

As he starts to get up, CHARLES *clambers on top of him, attempting to kiss him.*

(*Struggling to push him off.*) Dear God, Charles!…

He manages to shove CHARLES *off, who then lands with a bump on the floor.*

Get a grip, for Christ's sake!

The exertion has left them both breathless.

Leaping around like that! You'll bring on your angina.

CHARLES. I know how to look after myself.

HARRY (*keeping his voice down*). What the hell are you playing at anyway?

CHARLES. What we've always played at.

HARRY. Someone might come in!

CHARLES *awkwardly attempts to get to his feet.*

(*Offering a hand.*) Let me give you a hand.

CHARLES (*roughly knocking it away*). Keep it to yourself!

With great effort he finally succeeds, and stands for a moment getting his breath back.

HARRY. Do you want some water?

CHARLES. No, I bloody don't!

He sits heavily on the other end of the sofa from HARRY. *Pause. The sound of digging continues.*

I thought that's what you liked, an element of danger: parks, lavatories, the club library –

HARRY. Alright!

CHARLES. On the sofa in your house with Fleur and Monty upstairs.

HARRY. Alright, alright!

CHARLES. But not any more, it seems.

HARRY. No, not any more.

CHARLES. A pity.

HARRY. Well, that's the way it is.

HARRY *checks the coast is clear.*

(*Still sotto voce.*) Tidy yourself up, for God's sake.

Beat.

CHARLES. I've danced to your tune for years, always been there when you wanted, made myself scarce when you didn't.

HARRY. Turn it down, will you!

CHARLES. I took you for an honourable man but now I'm not so sure.

HARRY. Come on, Charles. The spark goes out eventually. It's a fact of life.

CHARLES. But we've been through so much together – a bloody war, for Christ's sake! It's what we fought for.

HARRY. This doesn't become you.

CHARLES. You can't just push me away.

HARRY. Quite unseemly.

CHARLES. How the tables turn! There was a time you couldn't keep your hands off.

HARRY. Things are as they are and that's an end to it.

CHARLES. I have no one, Harry.

HARRY. You're starting to sound like Celia Johnson. Pull yourself together, man. Tighten up.

CHARLES *stares at him coldly and brushes himself down.* HARRY *pours himself another drink. Pause.* HARRY, *his back to* CHARLES, *is suddenly still. He clears his throat.*

CHARLES *glances at him.*

You were asking if something was up. Well, as it happens… there is. (*Checking again that the coast is clear.*) It's the firm. I've invested a hell of a lot recently, expanding and what-have-you, and soon, of course, it will start bringing in the bacon, but what with that and Monty's school fees… The fact is, old sausage, I'm stony.

BASIL, *half-dressed, enters.*

BASIL. Do you think we'll all fit in the Morris?

HARRY. If you'll excuse me.

He leaves the room.

CHARLES (*following* HARRY *out*). I just need to…

BASIL. Oh.

He stands there for a moment at a loss, then lights a cigarette, goes to the trolley and pours himself a Scotch. He wanders over to the French window and looks out, sipping his drink and smoking. The digging continues. ISABELLA *enters.*

ISABELLA. I wondered where you'd got to.

BASIL (*turning to her, arms outstretched*). Ah, butterfly! My clouded yellow!

ISABELLA. Basil, you know you're not very good with Scotch.

BASIL. How lovely you look!

They embrace.

Sometimes I have to pinch myself – in the car, the street, at work.

ISABELLA. You're not falling asleep on the job, are you?

BASIL. No, no –

ISABELLA. You work too hard, you know.

BASIL. It's because I can't believe my luck, the two of us, together.

ISABELLA. Oh my darling. I was telling Charles just now how happy I am.

BASIL. And sometimes I dare to imagine you and me – and the children.

ISABELLA. Let's not jump the gun.

BASIL. Even grandchildren as we grow old together.

ISABELLA. Old? Goodness! Why not get dinner out of the way first? (*Stroking his cheek*.) You're such a dear man. A dear, dear man.

She kisses him. He gently touches her stomach.

BASIL. Should we call him Charles as a special thank-you for the house?

ISABELLA. I don't think so.

BASIL. Then what about Joan, if it's a little girl, in honour of your mother?

ISABELLA. Oh heavens, no! That's a ghastly name.

BASIL. So what does my fair Isabella suggest?

ISABELLA. Have you ordered the taxi?

BASIL. I thought we'd take the Morris.

ISABELLA. Oh no, Basil, I am not arriving at Le Caprice in a Morris Minor. We'll take a taxi, so please, darling, get a move on and book it, there's a good boy.

BASIL *pecks her cheek*.

BASIL. My angel.

He leaves the room. ISABELLA *stands quite still for a moment, then rushes around the room flapping her hands and arms trying to get rid of his smoke. She stops and breathes deeply. She takes a cigarette, lights it and drags on it voraciously. She stubs it out and leans against the mantelpiece panting, her hand on her chest trying to control her breathing, then wanders over to a table and leans over it, head hung down. 'La Marseillaise' from the opening of The Beatles' 'All You Need Is Love' starts playing as the lights go down.*

Scene Three

BASIL (*forty-eight*) *alone on the sofa watching 'All You Need Is Love' being performed on the television. He's casually dressed. A warm June evening. The doors of the French window are closed.*

The unpacked boxes from the previous scene have now gone but the room is still none too tidy.

The latest Dansette record player stands on the table next to the twenties gramophone cabinet, discs piled around. After a minute or so, ISABELLA (*mid-thirties*) *busily enters, putting on earrings, dressed to go out. She throws open the French window and breathes in the air, the late golden sunlight streaming in, then goes to the drinks trolley and pours herself a gin. She takes a swig, then turns off the television before the song has finished.* BASIL *glances at her, then back at the blank screen. From outside, the occasional birdsong and rustling of trees.* ISABELLA *sits away from him and starts putting on a pair of shoes, which she's picked up off the floor.*

BASIL. That was the first ever live global television link.

No reply.

It's done via satellite.

ISABELLA *gets up, shoes on, sips her drink and goes over to the Dansette. She starts shuffling through some records.*

They estimate about four hundred million people will be watching that in twenty-six countries. It's hard to imagine, isn't it?

She chooses a record and takes it from its sleeve.

Four hundred million in twenty-six countries!

She puts the disc on the turntable.

(*Re: the blank screen.*) All sorts of people are there in the studio, singing along, clapping…

She puts the stylus on the disc.

Mick Jagger, Keith Moon. Very jolly…

His voice is drowned out by some very loud jazz: 'Baden-Baden' by The Modern Jazz Quartet. He glances at her again as she makes her way to the fireplace, moving to the music, to check herself in the mirror above the mantelpiece. She lights a cigarette, goes to the French window, leans against a jamb and smokes.

BASIL *waits for a moment, then gets up in his own time, goes over to the Dansette, takes the stylus off the disc and stands there.* ISABELLA *doesn't react, just carries on drinking and smoking, looking out at the garden. Silence. She throws down her cigarette and grinds it underfoot.*

ISABELLA (*sotto voce*). Do you know how difficult it was to tell you? Do you have any idea?

Beat.

I thought you might show something: a flare of anger, perhaps, fury, regret. I thought you might have a row, at least a discussion, reasoned or not, even a question.

BASIL *remains quite still.*

(*Turning on him.*) But you sat there saying – (*Suddenly yelling.*) nothing! Nothing! Just sat there and said nothing!

She stares at him, breathing fast.

BASIL. I might be mistaken, but you look at me sometimes as if you hate me.

Pause.

ISABELLA. No, you're not mistaken. The truth is, I can't endure you, but I do because I have to.

BASIL (*re: his clothes*). I'd better change.

ISABELLA. Yes, you better had.

> *The doorbell rings. He goes out.* ISABELLA *quickly checks herself in the mirror. From the hallway:*

BASIL. Uncle Charlie!

CHARLES. Basil, old chap.

BASIL. Come through, come through…

> CHARLES (*now sixty-eight), and* BASIL *enter.*

ISABELLA (*the perfect hostess*). Charles, how lovely!

CHARLES. What a peach you look!

> *They kiss.*

And the perfect evening for a bite by the river.

BASIL. Isn't it though?

ISABELLA. You're looking very dashing, Charles.

CHARLES. Get away with you! Do you really think so?

BASIL. Scotch?

ISABELLA. I'll get it. You get dressed.

BASIL. Right, I'll…

> *He goes out.* ISABELLA *pours a Scotch and a gin for herself.* CHARLES *looks out at the garden.*

CHARLES. Yes, a golden evening.

ISABELLA. It is.

CHARLES. When are you going to get your terrace done?

ISABELLA. It would be nice, wouldn't it?

CHARLES. And the garden could do with a short back and sides.

ISABELLA. Yes, but you wouldn't believe how hard it is to find a man.

CHARLES. Oh, I would, believe me. You should try and get hold of that chap who laid it out originally.

ISABELLA (*handing him his drink*). Cheers.

CHARLES. Cheers.

They drink.

Where's Barry?

ISABELLA. At my mother's.

CHARLES. Nice little fellow.

He takes out a packet of untipped cigarettes and offers her one.

No tipped, I'm afraid.

ISABELLA (*taking one*). Who cares?

CHARLES. That's my girl.

He lights hers, then his, and looks back out at the garden.

ISABELLA. Would you like some music or…?

CHARLES. An evening like this… It's music enough.

He inhales deeply. She smokes more nervously, pacing a little.

ISABELLA. Oh Charles, I've had the most awful day.

CHARLES (*stepping from the window*). I'm sorry to hear that, my dear.

ISABELLA. Quite awful.

CHARLES. A good dinner, a few stiff drinks – that'll do the trick.

ISABELLA. You know, sometimes I feel you're the only person I can talk to.

CHARLES. I'm sure you can talk to Basil. He's quite a sensitive soul – always has been.

ISABELLA. So you say.

CHARLES. He's a kind man, Isabella. He loves you, I've no doubt.

ISABELLA. Yes, he's kind, and he loves me.

CHARLES. And you must have friends you can talk to?

ISABELLA. I've found that since marrying and becoming
a mother –

CHARLES. And becoming a mother again.

ISABELLA. – you're rather left to get on with it, as if you're
perfectly able to cope, and this neighbourhood – it's not the
friendliest.

*She's wandered over to the French window and sips her
drink as she looks out at the garden, the golden sunset
casting her shadow across the room.* CHARLES *has sunk
into a chair.*

I never imagined I'd end up like this, you know: a wife and
mother. I always thought I'd have a career and independence.
At one stage I even contemplated engineering. I got hold of
course prospectuses and was convinced that this was where
my future lay. I told a friend at school who thought I was quite
mad, and even tried to discuss it with the headmistress –
I think she'd have been happier if I'd told her I was pregnant –
and when I told my father, he was furious. He said girls simply
didn't do that sort of thing, and no daughter of his was going
to be an engineer, and my mother of course always deferred to
him, and that put the final spanner in the works. He didn't
even want me to go to university. (*Re: the garden.*) You're
right, it could do with a tidy-up.

She swigs her drink. She hasn't looked at CHARLES, *who's
staring at the floor.*

I bumped into someone I knew earlier this year – well, I say
bumped; it wasn't quite like that. I was sitting in a café and
he walked past. I'd met him some years before. We'd only
spoken briefly – that's more or less all we did, all we could
do – but they were the few moments in life I really lived; the
rest has been just time passing. I left the café and went after
him – quite undignified, I must say – and for a second I don't
think he recognised me, but then he did, and he took me to
a seedy guesthouse off the Edgware Road. We made love on

the greasy sheets – well, a kind of love – and that was it. He had to get somewhere and so had I, but the point is, he's the father of the baby I'm carrying. You see, these days, Basil and I hardly ever make love, and when we do I take precautions; easy enough as he's never been too inquisitive in that department.

The dusky sunlight has turned golden-red.

Before you came, I told him. I had to. And he didn't react. He didn't say anything. If only he'd hit the roof, or me! But he just sat there, allowing it, and somehow, Charles, that makes it so much worse.

She finally looks at him. His head's slumped forwards. She shakes her head with a sigh.

(*Under her breath.*) What the hell?

She looks up at the sky and closes her eyes. A gentle rustling of the trees.

Mm… So warm… I wonder if it'll be a good summer? (*Turning to him.*) Charles? Charles!

She rushes to him and lifts his head. He tries to speak.

God, I thought you'd… What's wrong? What's wrong, Charles?

She holds him.

Oh Charles, I wouldn't have told you if I thought it was going to upset you so much.

CHARLES….I think…

ISABELLA. What?

CHARLES….I think I killed him.

ISABELLA. Who?

CHARLES. Harry. I think I killed Harry.

ISABELLA. Of course you didn't kill Harry. He jumped under a train.

CHARLES. Yes, but he –

ISABELLA. The District Line at Parsons Green. Everyone knows that. Of course you didn't kill him.

CHARLES. He left a note.

ISABELLA. A note? We don't know that, Charles. Nothing was ever found.

CHARLES. We do now. Monty found it. Monty, for God's sake! He's only fifteen! He was going through some junk the other day and there it was. Harry had decided to do away with himself because he was being blackmailed.

ISABELLA. Blackmailed?

CHARLES. Oh Isabella, you must know what he got up to. He always had an eye out for the chaps. He said how he'd lied, how he was a worthless husband and father, how the guilt had worn him down and he'd had enough. Imagine, reading that about your father, and poor old Fleur, believe it or not, she didn't have a clue. She told me all this yesterday. She's devastated. She thought he was just depressed.

ISABELLA. Couldn't he have gone to the police?

CHARLES. Not then. It would've been far too risky.

ISABELLA. Better that than…

CHARLES. If only he'd hung on! Things are somewhat different now, but… Stupid man! I knew something was wrong. I challenged him about it, but he never let on.

ISABELLA. But why on earth do you say you killed him?

CHARLES. He was broke. He lied and said it was because of what he'd invested in the firm, but of course now we know it was the blackmail which did for him. He begged me for money – it was that evening we were going to Le Caprice, remember? – shortly after you'd moved in.

ISABELLA. Yes, I do.

CHARLES. And because I was in a pet about… this and that… I didn't give him a penny, but if I had have, he'd still be here now.

ISABELLA. You don't know that for sure. You can't possibly take responsibility.

CHARLES. But one can't help wondering.

ISABELLA. You're being far too hard on yourself.

CHARLES. Do you think so?

ISABELLA. Of course you are.

CHARLES. Really?

ISABELLA. Yes!

CHARLES. Well, that's a relief.

ISABELLA. You're the kindest man in the world.

CHARLES. I wouldn't go quite that far.

ISABELLA. Believe me.

She clinks his glass. They drink.

Do they have any idea who the blackmailer was?

CHARLES. Some thug he probably picked up in an alleyway. Apparently he made him pay for favours, to put it delicately, and if he didn't, he'd have exposed him, which simply wouldn't do for a solicitor of his standing. Oh, the vanity of us all, but when the blood's up… I do miss him. I always will.

ISABELLA. Poor Charles.

She embraces him. BASIL*'s appeared, now dressed for dinner, watching. They haven't noticed him.*

BASIL. It's getting on.

ISABELLA *and* CHARLES, *startled, break the embrace.*

CHARLES. Oh Basil, old boy… (*Getting up, patting his hair, checking his tie.*) We were just…

BASIL. Time we left. We might lose the table otherwise.

CHARLES. Popular place, yes.

ISABELLA *goes to the mirror to check her hair and make-up.*

You're very good to me, you two, taking an old duffer with you here, there and everywhere.

ISABELLA. We enjoy your company, Charles. I'm not sure what we'd do without it.

BASIL. Shall I take the Mini or – ?

CHARLES. The Rover's roomier, don't you think?

ISABELLA. Oh yes. We can't go in the Mini.

BASIL. But Uncle Charles might prefer to –

CHARLES. We'll take the Rover. Quite happy to, old chap.

BASIL. Right. Thank you.

CHARLES. I'll tidy up the back seat.

He goes out, stranding BASIL *and* ISABELLA. *Beat.*

BASIL. Should we perhaps phone your mother? See how Barry is?

ISABELLA. No need. He'll be in bed by now.

BASIL. Yes of course. No need to phone.

Beat.

Then I'll just…

He doesn't move.

Lucky, aren't we?

She looks at him.

Your mother – always willing to take him.

ISABELLA. She spoils him.

BASIL. She dotes on him.

ISABELLA. It's inappropriate.

Beat. He turns to leave. Almost as an afterthought:

BASIL (*without looking at her*). I love you, Isabella – you do know that, don't you? – and I would never stop you from doing what makes you happy. We must all make the most of this life; it's short enough, God knows.

He goes out. She looks after him as the lights fade and the 'Act II pas de deux' from Tchaikovsky's The Nutcracker *fades in. Lights up on:*

Scene Four

The room is in exactly the same state as Scene One, the evening of that day. The rain has stopped. The only light is from the moon and the television, which BARRY's *watching on the sofa, the Tchaikovsky continuing (he's listening to it on his iPod). Just outside the open doors of the French window,* ISABELLA (*seventy-five*) *sits looking at the garden, drink in hand, smoking a cigarette; although facing away from the room, she seems to be aware of what's going on. When the music finishes, silence, except for the television (a programme about antiques).* BARRY *removes his earphones and adjusts his position as if in some discomfort. He continues staring at the screen. A sudden gurgling from upstairs pipes goes unremarked. Pause.*

BARRY. You'll catch your death.

Beat.

It's cold.

ISABELLA. It's summer.

BARRY adjusts his position again.

You're fidgety tonight. Have you been up to something while I was in Dunstable?

Beat.

All this time on your hands: it isn't healthy. You're a sly boy.

BARRY. Boy!

ISABELLA. And lazy.

BARRY. I've been made redundant.

ISABELLA. You always were sly and lazy.

BARRY. Why don't you come in and shut the doors?

ISABELLA. And no balls to speak of – just like your father. Balls, *cojones*, that's what you need.

BARRY. I'm trying to watch television.

ISABELLA swigs her drink and lights a new cigarette from the old one, which she flicks into the darkness.

ISABELLA. If you were normal you'd be kicking them around, whacking them with a bat or knocking them into holes or… bouncing them off your head. Or scratching them. I don't think I've ever seen you scratch yours.

BARRY (*sotto voce*). Jesus Christ.

ISABELLA. Just like your father.

BARRY. You've drunk too much.

ISABELLA. Always the same; you always had to be different. Never mucked in with the other boys.

BARRY. You were never there to cheer me on.

ISABELLA. You did nothing to cheer, just pranced around on the periphery. If only you were more like Monty.

BARRY. Monty's gay.

ISABELLA. So you say.

BARRY. Like father, like son – except Monty's more honest about it.

ISABELLA. Sporty, tough, everything a young man should be.

BARRY. He's over sixty!

He subtly readjusts his position; she catches him.

ISABELLA. See? You have been up to something.

He ignores her. The grating, cranking of the fridge. She stares up at the night sky. He continues watching television. The cranking stops.

(*Holding out her glass.*) Plop a gin in there, will you?

BARRY. You've had enough.

ISABELLA. Gin!

He gets up, goes over to her and takes the glass. As he pours a drink at the trolley:

BARRY. Mind you, I can't see Monty topping himself like his dad did, even though his partner has just left him and seems to be taking him to the cleaner's. The way people behave! (*Going back to her with the drink.*) Odd, isn't it? It used to be funerals all the time, then civil partnerships, now it's divorces.

Her head's lolled forward; she's dropped off. He places the drink beside her and returns to the television. He eases himself down onto the sofa and watches. A police siren passes, then fades into the distance.

ISABELLA (*muttering to herself in a reverie*).…My baby. My beautiful boy… (*Coming to a little, raising her head.*) I was sitting just here, on this very spot, staring at the stars, lost in a dream, with little Laurence asleep in his cot beside me.

BARRY*'s continuing to watch television; he's obviously heard all this before.*

A stifling, midsummer night, and the bedroom… so hot. Basil snoring like a donkey, and you in the boxroom dead to the world. But down here was so peaceful, the air slightly cooler, just myself and my baby, and I lit a joint and drifted off, I can't tell for how long, but when I came to – (*Becoming tearful.*) he was gone. I hoped I was imagining it, that it was a dream… How could he do it to me? He'd wanted me to run away with him, promised me that one day I'd have his baby and he was right. But when he suddenly turned up here some while later, and I insisted it wasn't his… well, of course, he knew… and I lost them both.

Beat.

I dream of him sometimes, my little Laurence, what he was like, what he might be like now… what I'll say to him when he comes back…

BARRY (*not taking his eyes off the television*). And how is that going to happen?

ISABELLA. There are more things in heaven and earth –

BARRY. Mothers always think their children will return but they hardly ever do.

ISABELLA. That's a cruel thing to say. He was my son, my baby!

BARRY (*engaging with her*). You've tried everything, Mother, even contacting the spirit world in Dunstable! But you have to accept things as they are. It's hard, but there it is – and you do still have a son who loves you.

ISABELLA. You're a chump!

He turns his attention back to the television. She swigs her drink and stares up at the stars. Pause.

By the way, there's a bloodstain on the sofa.

BARRY (*thrown*). Is there? I haven't noticed.

ISABELLA. On the arm next to you.

BARRY (*glancing at the arm*). Oh that! (*Unconvincingly.*) It's been there ages.

ISABELLA. It wasn't there this morning. You're not even a good liar.

Beat.

Chump.

Pause.

(*Her speech now quite slurred.*) What's for supper?

BARRY. We've had it.

ISABELLA. I fancy Melba toast with a big blob of faux pas.

BARRY. Foie gras.

ISABELLA. Just the ticket.

BARRY. You've drunk too much.

ISABELLA. Why don't you give me something nice instead of the usual muck?

Her head lolls to the side; she's dropped off again. A brief, dying gurgle of the upstairs pipes. BARRY *continues watching television, lit by its flickering images and the moonlight.*

BARRY (*eyes fixed on the screen*). You won't leave me, will you? Please don't leave me.

ISABELLA (*back in her reverie*). My angel… My sweet boy…

Morten Lauridsen's 'O Magnum Mysterium' sung by Norwich Cathedral Choir starts playing as the lights fade.

Scene Five

The room as in Scene Two, the moment after. ISABELLA (*late twenties*) *is leaning over the table, her head hanging down, the late golden sunlight, now tinged with red, streaming through the French window. A* GARDENER (*late thirties*) *silently appears at the French window, silhouetted in the dusky golden-red light, and leans against a jamb watching her. At first she doesn't notice him, then turns with a start.*

ISABELLA. Oh!

GARDENER. Sorry. I didn't mean to –

ISABELLA. What?

GARDENER. Startle you.

ISABELLA. No.

Beat.

GARDENER. It's just that I've –

ISABELLA. Finished, have you?

GARDENER. Yes, and Mr Pritchard –

ISABELLA. Pritchard?

GARDENER. Harry.

ISABELLA. Oh, Harry!

GARDENER. Yes, he told me you'd be going out.

ISABELLA. We're going for dinner to Le Caprice.

GARDENER. Ooh, that's nice. Bit of French.

ISABELLA. Yes.

He watches her, making her self-conscious.

Have you known him long?

GARDENER. Not really. We met through a mate over a jar. He needed a job doing, then he got me a few more. Good bloke, Harry.

ISABELLA. Yes, he is.

Beat.

GARDENER. Was that you on the old joanna?

ISABELLA. Oh… no. That was the gramophone. We don't have a – piano.

The GARDENER *steps inside. As he saunters over to the gramophone:*

It was an 'Étude'. By Chopin.

GARDENER. An 'Étude', eh? Well. Do you like Elvis, Mrs Gough?

ISABELLA. I suppose I do.

GARDENER. He's the king, he is, young Elvis. (*Stroking the gramophone.*) This has seen some service, I bet. Twenties, isn't it?

ISABELLA. Probably.

GARDENER. You should get your hubby to buy you a Dansette. Lovely little numbers. You can get them that you can carry around and that.

ISABELLA. Oh.

GARDENER. Not like this old thing. Don't get me wrong, it's alright for what it is, but it's a bit – ungainly, isn't it?

ISABELLA. It does keep sticking and – slipping and sliding.

GARDENER. That's no good, is it? Sticking and slipping and sliding. You won't find a Dansette doing that. No, they're lovely little numbers.

ISABELLA. Yes, you said.

Beat.

Well, I have to…

GARDENER. Course you do – if you're going to Le Caprice. Is that your Rover outside?

ISABELLA. No, I'm afraid not.

GARDENER. She's a beauty. Which one's yours then?

ISABELLA. The Morris Minor.

GARDENER. Right. I've always fancied a sporty Merc myself. One day. Who knows?

Muffled voices from another part of the house. A door shutting. Silence.

ISABELLA. I really must –

GARDENER. Now how's that for a sunset?

She looks out at the golden-red light.

You'd be hard pushed to get that down on canvas.

ISABELLA. Yes.

GARDENER. I like this time of day, with night just round the corner. I love the night, Mrs Gough.

ISABELLA. Do you?

GARDENER. That's when our real hearts beat, under cover of darkness. I saw you just now, all by yourself, flapping around the room.

ISABELLA. You've no business spying on me!

GARDENER. I just happened to look up, that's all. You didn't look very happy, Mrs Gough – if you don't mind my saying.

ISABELLA. I do mind your saying, actually. I think you're rather impertinent.

GARDENER. Sorry. Didn't mean to offend. That's my trouble: can't keep it shut.

She lights a cigarette as he leans against the window looking out, and starts singing quietly to himself a few lines of Elvis Presley's 'It's Now or Never'.

ISABELLA *glances at the door to the rest of the house, then at him. She drags on her cigarette.*

ISABELLA. I feel trapped sometimes, that's all.

He stops singing.

At home I did, at school – and now. I think I know what I want but then life dishes up something quite different, and to get through, you convince yourself that's what you wanted all along. You have to, don't you? Else you'd go mad.

GARDENER. I think you should take what you want when you want, that's what I reckon. It's over in a minute; there's no time to fanny around. We don't have the first idea, Mrs Gough, none of us. We're just tiny little grains on a tiny little planet in a tiny little system. There's other worlds out there, worlds of wonder, but this is our lot, so better make the most of it. (*Looking out.*)

ISABELLA*'s now next to him.*

The kind old sun, nearly gone.

ISABELLA. I think I'd better –

GARDENER. Listen!

ISABELLA. What?

GARDENER. That bird…

Silence.

ISABELLA. I can't hear anything.

GARDENER. A nightingale.

ISABELLA. I don't think so.

GARDENER. It is. Listen.

Only silence.

ISABELLA. There's nothing there.

GARDENER. It's a nightingale, Mrs Gough.

ISABELLA. You've a most poetic nature.

GARDENER. A nightingale. It was.

Beat.

ISABELLA. You can call me Isabella, you know.

GARDENER. I don't want you thinking I'm not a gent, Mrs
  Gough.

He embraces her and kisses her with passion.

One day you'll be carrying my baby. Would you like that?

She stares at him.

I promise.

They kiss again.

Come with me.

ISABELLA. What?

GARDENER. Slip out the gate, easy as pie.

ISABELLA. Why would I want to do that?

*A distant church bell starts playing 'The Angelus Hymn' as
he pushes up the skirt of her dress and puts his hand between
her legs. Their embrace becomes more intense, then subsides
as 'The Angelus' ends.*

(*Quietly.*) I can't.

BASIL (*from another part of the house*). Izzy! Izzy!

She leaves the room. The GARDENER *reflects for a
moment, lights a cigarette, then stands at the French window
and looks out at his handiwork.* HARRY *enters.*

GARDENER. All done, Mr Pritchard.

He's about to discard his cigarette.

HARRY. No, you enjoy your smoke. You deserve it.

GARDENER. Thank you, Mr Pritchard.

HARRY (*looking out*). Good work. Yes, jolly good work.

GARDENER. You know me, Mr Pritchard. You can always rely
on me.

HARRY. Yes. Reliable. I like that.

GARDENER. Always do what I say I will.

HARRY. Yes, yes, I know.

Beat.

GARDENER. Scrubbed up well, Mr Pritchard. (*Inhaling.*) Mm.
You smell lovely. All fresh and clean.

HARRY (*checking they're alone*). Little bit of a hitch.

GARDENER. Oh dear. I'm sorry to hear that.

HARRY. But I will see you alright.

GARDENER. Will you?

HARRY. I always do, don't I?

BASIL *suddenly bursts in.*

BASIL. Harry, we're off! Oh, sorry…

HARRY. No, no, I was just… admiring his handiwork.

BASIL. Yes, splendid job…

GARDENER. Thank you, Mr Gough.

BASIL. Splendid.

GARDENER. A few more days should do it.

Beat.

Well, better get my stuff. Don't want to keep you gents from Le Caprice.

HARRY. No, that's right…

GARDENER. Very smart. I'd like to go there myself one of these days.

BASIL. I'm sure you will.

GARDENER. Ooh, I don't know about that, Mr Gough. We keep being told we've never had it so good, but I haven't seen any of it yet. (*Chuckling.*) Have I, Harry?

HARRY. No, but as Mr Gough says, I've no doubt you will.

GARDENER. D'you reckon?

HARRY. You're the sort of chap that usually get what he wants, aren't you?

CHARLES (*off*). Where the hell has everyone got to?

HARRY (*calling*). We're coming!

As HARRY *turns to go:*

GARDENER. I'll call you tomorrow, then, Mr Pritchard.

HARRY. Yes.

GARDENER. I could pop round your house –

HARRY. No.

GARDENER. Or your office, if that'd be more convenient.

HARRY. A telephone call would be preferable.

GARDENER. Whatever you want, Mr Pritchard.

HARRY. Yes. Thank you.

He goes, leaving the two of them together, BASIL *feeling a little self-conscious. Pause.*

BASIL. Glorious evening.

GARDENER. Quite special, I'd say.

BASIL. Isn't it though?

GARDENER. Better get packing.

BASIL. You carry on.

Neither of them move. Pause.

GARDENER. Looking forward to being a dad then, Mr Gough?

BASIL. Oh. Yes, I suppose I am.

GARDENER. You're a lucky man. It's what I've always wanted, a kid.

BASIL. Really?

GARDENER. More than anything.

BASIL. I thought it was women who got broody.

GARDENER. Seeing him grow, whether he'll be like you, look like you. The best gift in the world.

BASIL. Put like that…

GARDENER. As I say, Mr Gough, you're a lucky man. You make the most of it.

He goes into the garden, BASIL *watching him. Beat. The sound of a taxi pulling up.*

BASIL (*lurching back to reality and checking his watch*). Oh God!

He rushes out. The stage is empty as we hear the sound of doors opening and closing, muffled voices, and the taxi engine. Then ISABELLA *appears. She goes to the French window and looks out expectantly; it's obvious no one's there. She looks back into the room, then out again at the garden, silhouetted in twilight.*

(*Off.*) Izzy! Izzy!

ISABELLA (*calling*). Yes, I'm coming!

She's about to close the French window when she suddenly hears something: a nightingale. She stands stock-still. The nightingale sings. She listens as the lights fade.

The End.

A Nick Hern Book

Twilight Song first published in Great Britain as a paperback original in 2017 by Nick Hern Books Ltd, The Glasshouse, 49a Goldhawk Road, London W12 8QP, in association with Park Theatre, London

Twilight Song copyright © 2017 The Estate of Kevin Elyot

Kevin Elyot has asserted his moral right to be identified as the author of this work

Cover photography by Oliver Rosser for Feast Creative

Designed and typeset by Nick Hern Books, London
Printed in the UK by Mimeo Ltd, Huntingdon, Cambridgeshire PE29 6XX

A CIP catalogue record for this book is available from the British Library.

ISBN 978 1 84842 681 8

Woodland
CARBON
www.woodlandcarbon.co.uk
NICK HERN BOOKS
Printed on Carbon Captured paper